ONWARDS

By the same author

Cherish: WWI ANZAC Poetry

Onwards

Poems for life's departure

P. A. WATKINS

Foreword by Rod MacLeod

Sóþfæstnysse Press
PO Box 3246, Whangārei 0142

A catalogue record for this book is available
from the National Library of New Zealand

First published 2021

© P. A. Watkins 2021
All rights reserved

The moral rights of the author have been asserted

ISBN: 978-0-473-60278-9 (Hardback)
ISBN: 978-0-473-60277-2 (Paperback)

This book is copyright. Except for the purposes of fair reviewing no part of this publication may be reproduced or transmitted in any form or by any means, electronic or mechanical, including photocopying, recording or by any information storage or retrieval system, without permission in writing from the publisher.

*For Sunday,
sister amongst stars,
shining!*

Contents

Foreword	*i*
Acknowledgements	*iii*
Give Way	*1*
Enfold	*3*
Summer Rays	*5*
Shine	*7*
Change	*9*
So Be	*11*
Heartscape	*13*
Our Holy Night	*15*
Tidal	*17*
Inward Search	*19*
Here and Now	*23*
Wait	*25*
Goodwill	*27*
Turbulence	*29*
Moonlight Sonata	*31*
Beyond	*33*
Old Day	*35*
I Weep	*37*
Farewell	*39*
In Time	*41*
Renew	*43*
Full Circle	*45*
Strandline	*49*
Know Thyself	*51*
Growth	*53*
Our Thread	*55*
Golden Memory	*57*
Known	*59*
Fade Away	*61*
Release	*63*
Towards	*65*
One	*67*

Loose Ends	69
Good Company	73
Intersection	75
Perspective	77
Song of Peace	79
Deliverance	81
Light Shaft	83
Renewed	85
Unstitched	87
Again	89
Good Fruit	91
Uncertainty	93
On Time	95
Canvas	99
Out of Depth	101
More Time	103
In Love	105
Begin	107
To Be	109
Heart's Heart	111
Awaiting	113
Into	115
Gauge	117
Becoming	119
Hollow	121
I	123
Enough	127
Departure	129
Dear One	131
All's Well	133
Open	135
Horizons	137
Antiphon	139
Flow	141
Set	143
Slip Switch	145
Call	147
To Dream	149

Photography

Brians101 via Getty Images: Cover
Mexitographer via Getty Images: pg 20-21
jessa2482 via Getty Images: pg 46-47
jplenio via Pixabay: pg 70-71
kordula vahle via Pixabay: pg 96-97
David Baileys via Getty Images: pg 124-125
Kerstin Riemer via Pixabay: pg 150-151

Foreword

Writing poems is a deeply personal activity. Reading them is often the same.

What shines through these verses is a gentle reflective spirit that encourages us to think about these carefully crafted words over and over. Some of them may give you reason to suddenly pause – *If all I hold is imagination/ Am I really living? ...* (Good Fruit) or *In memories shared/ My burden lightens/ In tears shed/ I am relief/ With hope's smallest sign/ My heart awakens ...* (All's Well) and, *And with, truth and love/ We ascend, when enough* (Enough).

Interspersed with images that give encouragement to think about what we have just read - you may find yourself going back to reread and review what these verses are saying to you. They urge us to stop and reflect, to think, and to value all that we have and at times, what we are going to lose.

In life's/ Golden/ End is/ Always/ Love

Rod MacLeod MNZM
Auckland, May, 2021

Acknowledgements

Thank you, to you - near, afar

Give Way

When tide's hold softens
My wings sigh

As sun-waves golden
My soul sways

As light sings salt's canon
My heart rings

In gentle jubilation given
My way opens

Enfold

Heart's lamp
Light with the oil of life
Carry soul, in comfort beyond
With burden's blessing laid to rest
And newborn release
Enfolded, in love's warm grace
Peace be,
Peace

Summer Rays

Gather in
Cords of time
Memory's linens
Woven breath

Breathe in joy
Capsules past
Textures of here and known

Gifting reflection
Granting redemption
In folds, of folds

Bringing to ear, warmth of sunlight
Brimming laughter
Ever there, ever same

Lightening to tears this young heart
Free from wrappings
Known to self

Now, as then, and again

Shine

When will the shine come?
I hold breath, and steel it in mysterious places
Caverns of self

Will I wait?
Watching for land's breath to yield hint of
  openings?

Will I find my way?
Crawling belly to squeeze this life, through
  these unknown cracks,
Mosaics of self.

Is this where the shine glimmers?
Floundering on some forgotten rock in some
  forgotten cavern?

I drift through these chambers
Touching all in review, in search, in complacency.
Instilling these smoky walls to conceal from self
This glimmer
There waiting,
Patiently
For sun's hour to soften all
In the flood of beginning

Pure shine

Change

In innocence
Lay, head to heart's tie
Bind in hope's arms
Fastened, firm

Quell limitation
In love's lattice
Founded on immortal streams
Of longing
And living

Across
And through
Beyond sticks and lines

Sands eternal

Be wind, at once
And new

So Be

I feel the wash and pull of time
Running out

This flicker of curtains
Soon to meet

The need and drive of necessities
Less essential

'stead wind-danced greenery, spring-soaked air
Hold
New intensity
New necessity
To notice, to grasp
To feel
The vast pull of sun
All and sundry
Woven, straight and true
Expansive, complete
Cognisant of each shade and light, tone and hue
Binding one with all
In compassed step
And yet

Sands continue
Seasons fall and rise
Necessarys demand

Such apparent contradiction
Detail, expanse
Pressure, release

How to move step rightly
On changeable ground
And direct will in time
To blend broadness and intensity
 purposefully, truly?

I cannot will beyond limb's
Each
Single
Step

So be it

Heartscape

Crystalline expanse
Shimmering memories
Warm jewels of hope
Carpeting heart
In dawn's glorious chorus

Subduing moments lost
Overcoming sorrows
Lightening life's burdens
In gilded dreams
Of acceptance
Of life's tomes and gifts

Above breath's foibles
Dissolving soul's rocks
To uncover glints of gold
And release
In time
Purpose fulfilled

Our Holy Night

Twining knit
Weave long
Leave forgotten dreams agone
Betoken, should the shining past
Keen the languid stream, held fast
In the grip, of silken wing
Fluttering time, past, new begin

Mulled in layers
Time betook
Stilled in waxen scene afoot
Wasting, wanting
Ever still
Movement of an untrained will

Chosen path of unknown glade
Shaded realm
Within long strayed
Note in hand
Yet chanced aken
This grist-strewn path
For strength within

Absent in
The critical hour
Lost the chance
To grow
To flower
Fuller with each breath of night
Bereft without this tonic's sight

Onwards pressing
To the shores
Of one's holy evermores
Pulling weights
'Til all's revealed
Left with weightless burdens healed

Moving on in earth's next test
Watching, waiting
With the rest

'Til this twine spins fine in cloth
Do we pass on
As the moth
Striving inward
Towards the light
In humble prayer
For our holy night

Tidal

I am the tide
Surging, retreating

Scuttling shell
To roll magnetic

Flashing white wing
In sky's canvas

Sublime, fracturing
Becalmed, illumined
Dark, unremitting

Full of life

Inward Search

Soft clarity
Reaching
Direct

Boundless certainty
Loving truth

Still awareness
Patient acceptance

Ever present
Inward search

Here and Now

I once was
And did

I saw
And it was different

I see
Then, now

I am
And I will be

Wait

Wait for me
Wait

Pull rugsack to comfort
Clasped in air's hold
Challenging release

To wait

For,
Then see
For feel, feel to see

To find, thread, for carpet's place
Lain in time, gone
Returned

Loom's latch
In wait
In want, of a good yarn

Still, hibernating
Awaiting turn, warmth
Time

Wait

Goodwill

I strive for courage in vests of sky
And seek forgiveness in river's silts

I embrace love's fore kindnesses
And climb as shoot, indebted

I fill in hope heart's subtle rose
And flow with air's forgiving free

I brook the basements of intellect's gall
And love openly each crack and flint

I shed as past my fear of fall
And dissolve lament in warmth's fine kernel

I give to earth graceful thanks
And fold in humility my place to till

I blossom gently with soul-tuned grace
And call in love, my duty done

Turbulence

Aloft
Buoyed in throws
Gusted, hollowed

In suspension

In fall
Inner fall
Falling freely
Fallen?

'buffed to slides
Up
Slip up? Fall
Caught, caught
Of current's whim

A throw, again

Moonlight Sonata

Turn back
Soft melody
Of light
Of old

Frame windows of journey's past
Aligning course
To true intent

Move, beat slow
Now concise.

How unusual the rhythm set by human
 hands and leaden feet, uncoupled,

Still, onwards, stale to fresh
Beating incessantly

Awaiting the guiding known
Of soft light
Mirroring intent, reflecting action, making us
Anew

If ears and feet would listen

Beyond

Hour's glass
Immaterial

On wings
Beyond time
Soars soul

Dissolving glass, to sand
To dust
To breath
To beam, of light
Of soul
Beyond

Old Day

This torment
Is the final lament
The echoing
Of sun's descend

Where curved glint
Flashes
And sinks, rapidly
Landing on some
Hidden floor
Of time

Resounding in
Resolution
And grief

Tolling
For another day
Lost

I Weep

I weep for you
Rivers to oceans
I weep

Raining as thoughts
In squall
I weep

Raining as memories
In sun
Showering my soul
In resilience

In love
I weep

Farewell

Hand in hand
Silence

Oceans wash
Leaving their cast
Between and upon us

Eye to eye
Flickering wave, salting face in new streams
  to taste

Fingers lock in
This love, so firm
Withstanding

Crest to air, rock to smile
Dancing bells of laughter
Gust to salt, sea to wind
Heart and string, taut, free

Our clasp holds, she slips through
Joining these salty currents
Blurring us together

Salt, sea, chimes, love
Tears, blessings, gone

In Time

Turn in time
Wonderous past
Awakening inner peace

Go on, to know
Time's stillness

Turn again
Find anew

Day to night
Beautiful still

Renew

Memory's shadows
Caul to self
Hiding the hidden
Clearly

Slough midnight's cocoon
To wing
As love
Through night

Breathe air
To heart's knot
Funneling grain's folds
To mend in kisses
This limb lost

And gently
Allow dawn's slipper
To touch
And bring brow to shine
In sigh's new light

Full Circle

To love, love's embrace
Full circle

Drawing back tides of hair and sweat and soil
Turmoil, birth and hate

Stone-filled mounds
Sun-bound minds

Within the soul
A yearning
"Forthwith I lie"
"Not this, not this!"

To love's balm soften
Embrace
Full circle

Wing

as love

through light

Strandline

Purposefully, each step's spread
Loves these familiar sands
Glistening grains of futures past
Glittering remnants of times fulfilled

My eye meets shell after shell
Monuments of life's each moment
Laid long along this stretch

Wind strives with me
Humming through and releasing
Each shell's knowns

I harken intently to these intones
Charging air in an affray
Of this life's harmonics

Sounding and resounding
According, discording
Amassing ever and ever

Filling my ears
To lean in
Embracing all

Magnificent hum!
Remembered

Know Thyself

In heart, my head rests poorly
Pulled by designs of times
Machinations of expectations
Folly, to heart's self

In heart, my soul resounds, enlivened
Merging, in a wash of colour, and melody
Singing sweetness,
Flower through stem
Finding root
In heart,
My self

Growth

Beyond imagination
Step in
Merge light to sinew
Reality reviewed
Bridging façade to certainty
Met uncertainly

Digest to sustain
Meet anew
In step
Courage to view

Hides hidden
Reptilian
Upholstering familiars
Far gone

Cleanse in light's light
Bathe in strength
To shed
To hold
To release

Our Thread

Heart-sick wondering
Furlough friend
Ages between
A hand to extend

Willows for weeping
The loss of the years
Millions of missed
Hopes, joys, fears

Tears that are falling
Flow to the shore
Pulling me back
To you once more

Golden our friendship
Gilded on heart
Too strong to tear
Our thread weaved apart

Golden Memory

New light
Familiar

Time's turnkey
Swirl of wonder

Butter starlight
Sounds hummed
Spice, thought
Melody on heart

Open vistas
Splashed with colour

Where next?

Wonder
Swirling

Known

I awoke not knowing myself
As air and light, substance and time
Absent of that gravity of thought and feeling
That pulls and frays and pulls and sways upon
 intent

Rain runs streams down my heart
Sunlight bursts colour, to the edges of my mind

I sway to stay, to go
In joy and content
In sorrow and failure
I am all of this
Spinning
Still

Free in form
To fill new memories
Woven so close
Indistinguishable

Asleep, yet known to myself

Fade Away

Fade away my skylight scene
Above, beyond, abreast, between
Hollow sound, resonant within
The hiddenness, of everything

To dream a dream of rectitude
At once so close now far removed
A mind cast back to inward eye
No scope to blend, to bend, to cry
To question now and everything
Too conscripted to fall in
No meadows left to skim and breathe
The light-shone joy, the heart-strong weave
A mind now full of empty things
How does one staunched begin to sing?
And find a way back to the shores
Of inward calm, of evermore?

Too long the rope has leased me out
Upon a tireless wave of doubt
Of constant troughs and cast abouts
Of new moon tides and wordless shouts
Of a mind all too silent now
A head too prolonged in its bow

To rise again? This question must
To sail the storm, full-bodied bust
And find once more some piece within
The abstract puzzle of herein
Which once was sturdy, sound and whole
A glimpse of that is all now holds

And is this enough on its own
To guide the way, onward home?
And nuzzle once more, warm and sound
A wholesome, heartened soul unbound to
Endless fear and toil, all woe
The greatest of these
Thee must know
And knowledge now put to the test
Must first put heart within thy breast

Knowing full well that triumph of love
Is all that's needed from above

Release

Sigh in shed
These thoughts

Weighty clothing of
Mind's aggrievements

Part to bare
Eternal grain
Sloughed of seasons rings
True to shoot
Again

Tuning fall's blankets
To deepen roots
And filter purpose

In time
Lighter, gentler, softer
In warmth now

Towards

To grace I gift my soul

In light I hold my own

To love I direct my purpose

In truth I strive to find

One

In this afterglow
May I know
That I will see you all
Clearly
As we are
And have been
In joy,

Joyous reunion
In communion
With sun's wonders
Earthly
Heavenly

Flowing through
As colours soft, dappled
Splendid, resounding
Grounding heart
Freeing soul
To enfold
This grace of us all

Humming spheres
Effervescent
In clear thought
And love

Bound as one symphony
Eternally
Above, through
And beyond

Loose Ends

I am slowing down
Down
Long alleys, branching
To times, tanned in sun's touch

Touch
Faded feel,
Bright in heart's lens
Pointing to memories

Memories
Overlooked, significant
Frozen in tapestries
Hung in each opening

Open

Relive, in calm
Resolve, in understanding, and hope

Hope
In love's surety

Memory's linens

lightening to tears

this young heart

Good Company

To sit with you
Is to be.
Refreshed

Breathing air
Listening to our calm
Growing in our
Togetherness

Light, birds, waves, trees
Music merging
In the glory
Of our company

To be understood
By being
Is blessing
Beyond measure

Complete
Our otherworldly peace

Intersection

In between worlds I lie
Novice of one and t'other

Steady tick
Time turns
To past, to future, to necessity

I meet all at once
At end's intersection
Desperately tying loose threads
Triaging each's importance in want of time,
 energy
Gifted at this turn
By grace of departure

Hurried, relaxed
Stretch of time

Elasticity befriend!
And calm endow

May I do it well

Perspective

I am
As you are
And see
As you see

Frail and fading
Strong and clearer
Than ever
Before

Moving this
Inferior exterior
Through life's final adage

"Of this
We are
So much more"

Song of Peace

Make way
Straight
To mind.
Still as oceans
Supple as breath
Heart-kiss to soul-cheek
At peace

Make way
Straight
To soul.
Lived, in tone true
Mirroring mind's intent
One with heart's pull
Soul, full

Make way
Straight
To heart.
Sound, in water's touch
Founding soul's purpose
Through love's light shone
Heart, soul, song

Deliverance

Lonely days
Silence unbecoming
Stillness abounds
Settling as dust in want of sunlight

How too am I?
Vapid thought.
A drop in one's internal honour
That strength might fail thee thus

How much longer can one endure?
Inert as seed crowns, rent of their babes

The cloud of fear does not touch me
I see it, and its possibility

With the sun,
Rise to find solace
Of inner refinement
Through knowledge beyond capacity
And love
That knows no bounds

Light Shaft

Fall through, glassen sands
Silken layers
Shrouds of time
Billowing, and blessing
Nape to crown
Glorious auburns!

Warming blush
Shimmering

Reflecting blush
Warmth for warmth, all for all

Heartening and enwrapping
In shine's caress
To day
New
Through light

Renewed

Each hour, rings anew
As glossy leaf, as subtle dew
Which falls with touch, soft as light
Heralding new birth through night
Bringing forth remembered hope
Fresh, green, enlivened scene
Of inner truth, now spoke

Within the self of reasons been
Within the known of truths unseen
Within the heart, the soul of now
Within the why and here,
Somehow

That you'd forgot to live the life
You'd prepared, 'stead this sufficed

But now, within new clarity
The truth of it is plain, so be
Awakened once again, renewed
In memory's gift, now imbued
With journey's pearls and hardships balms
With honesty's reflective charms
To savour now in circle's meet
Renewed step in surety

Too late?

Never.

Unstitched

How to draw
This ache
Up from its hold?
Sewn to rib's innards
Tethered in hope, despair
Experience and dread

Can it be hewn
And lain to rest
Under some pillow
Or tree
Of memory?

Surely light can
Pull
To extract
This trial

I call for it
Everywhere
Feeling ever
That soon
Cloud will shift
And splendour arrive
Caressing me
To alight
Lightened
In dawn's good time
Drawn

Again

Behold, as child
Kindle heart's thread, to move in circles
Eclipsing time's reach
Ennobling patinaed paths

Stones to step
Each a leap
Of faith

Curving forward, glorious loops
Blending insights in rhythm
Known to heart, to inspiration

Acquiescing love
To prove love
And distill

Impregnating time
With harvests autumnal
Again, and again
In grace

Good Fruit

If all I hold is imagination
Am I really living?

If all I live is memory
Do I impart value?

If all I value is bygone
Can I relax in my comfort?

If my comfort is recollection
Did I ever matter?

If I am immaterial
Where do these rags lay?

If best laid plans fragment
May clemency resound
And branch to branch, wed this life
With heart and soul enwound

If life's fruits now must seed
Pray fertile ground they call
And wend strong roots in hope, in peace
Beyond the pale, to all

Uncertainty

Gone
On a breeze of doubt
That arrived subtly

I embodied the chill
After
As dirge
Drained of that liveliness
That animates the inanimate
With weathered soul, and engrained smile
And living quiet
Living stillness

Replaced now
Uncertain star

On Time

Tarry not, blend and be
Translucent, in this air of we
Wholesome glove, sound of fit
Guiding path beyond the quick

Tarry long, soul's urge sways
Blend in song this course of days
Holding dear to all since past
Long this glance of sunset's last

Tarry nay, for onwards need
Time to tie off
This life's weave
Never again will there be
Fabrics stitched the way did thee

May the true strings leave a thread
To build upon
In earth's next tread
For soon the glow of dawn's soft blessing
Will embrace
This sweet forgetting

Winter of soul

flow through me!

Canvas

Send in love your song
Breathing hues to paint
In fine
This roughed heart

Layer to layer
Smoothing life's ripples
To yield calm
To still place

To bleed and bleed
This heart

Out of Depth

Watery depths astride
Washing timbers
Narrow, true

Unseen pull, surges
Raising tides external
Attempting to breach the internal

Feel for plank, strive to carry forth
Over, it washes, sweeping, pushing
Lifting foot from board

Weightless

Connect, brief
Grasp to sight
Crawling, knees to board to shore

To turn from destruction,
A mighty thing.
To retrace,
A gift, a patient guide,
Weighting course
True to plumb, to spirit.

In surer seas
In time to come
Lose not this sight

More Time

My final hour
Was meant to be
Some joyous unknown

Not this
Slow waiting
Decrepit decaying

Am I not worth more
Than these long hours wasting,
Wasted on me?

Yesterday, that was.
Before this hour
Came
Beaming a picture
Of us
By the tree
Fuchsia
Crayon clad
Glowing off the page
Reflected in
Your bright
Spark
Smiling joy into
This hour
That I could never
Have known

Would that I
Now had more

In Love

Hold fast, immortal love
Light the path
Suffused, embracing

Lean onwards, held, fuller beat
Drowning outer shells of mortal truths

Upheld, in integrity of thought
True path
In light
In love

Onwards
Knowing good, giving right
Striving for hope
Living strength

Bend in love
Support in hope
Carry the chance, of growing
Onwards

Fulfilling the imagination of goodness
Within, without

Beaconing life, in unclothed glory
Beaming goodness
Through this world
And beyond

Begin

I cannot bleed

Thought a weighted veil
Inextricably bound
Dragging dusty memories
To air

Jettisoned
Aimlessly
Bombarding space
Fickle glint, settling
Illumination

Would 'druff from veil's enmeshing
Free, in light
Some hope
Some weight
That vein may yet fill
And chamber wring
Blood to beat, suspended

I yet may…

To Be

To hope for more,
and love for less

To build in wisdom,
and grow as light

To be

Heart's Heart

Woe betide
Stone-walled inside
Coppers cut
In a rut
Nothing comes
Insights numbed
Blinded, gummed
Intent undone

Plans unravelling
Proportions untethering
Heart's call wherefore?
Lost sight, offshore
Patience, in wait
So much at stake
To do or do not?
Hold back, or take shot?
Unfold what and where?
Await, and prepare?
For what, I don't know
Give way, let it show
Itself when time's right
So weather this blight
Until all's revealed
This new path to seal

But is it destination
This awaited revelation?
Or is waiting the test
To bring forth your best?

In meeting this challenge
By finding some balance
Towards light despite shade
Inner might wins the day
By overcoming shadows
And hardships and sorrows
To seek what is right
True intent towards light

Such depth of experience
May come from this weariness
And redoubt of one's mettle
In coursing life's nettles
Which times, hinder pathways
Requiring these crossways
And challenge direction
Suggesting correction
Or alternate avenues
To express one's other hues
And grow to explore
Self's depths to implore

Revival of purpose
Acceptance in service
Of one's higher self
You'd abandoned, in stealth
And move to a beat
New form feel and speech
That sings from the heart
And heralds the start
Of life lived as art
Dear heart!
Heart's heart

Awaiting

Time in wait
Arms swung still
Breath chancing release

Run, held fast
Planted, released
Seeking resolution, absolution, dissolution

A way forward
On solid ground?
Or harmonious air?

Winter of soul
Flow through me!

Into

Softly bend
Meekly yield
Flow in heart
To horizons

Expand thin line
And draw me into your unknown
Your vacuum

Suspended
Limitless
Unbound

Released to sky, to sea

Above, below, to and fro
At once
Complete
Given

Gauge

There is too much sorrow in this world
Dripping from eaves
Cementing to bone
Filling our shoes
Pouring over, splash to pool.

Some measure and compare
Their lots as watermarks
1 metre, 3 metres…
But what of it?

Better reckoning by far
The strength of light from ray
Or warmth of touch
Felt so keenly, so gratefully having known
Life's spring tides

Becoming

So long
This quiet
So long

Belonging to
The hour
The sun

My longing
To live
To love
To become

So quiet
This becoming

This long song

Hollow

I am nay
Here, astray
Wanderlust far gone
At bay?

Knocking corners
Tripping turns
Broken, fractured
Burnt, still it burns
Painfully on open moors
Gazing long abandoned shores

When did this depart from thee?
Blindly guttered
Shadowy

Grim, this husk of soul now hung
Absently
Within this one
Strained and foreign
Cast about
Clamoring
Now gone, no doubt

Hazy wisps, of before when
Light shone on the evermore
And though not clear within each step
Compassed, guided, free in check

Now these hollow bones of thought
Are all the memories left to sort

All that's left to rummage, pick
Dry sear bones to chew and knit
Into some semblance of a past
Into some picture that might last
The test of tattered memory's blinds
The pock-marked ground of battle's signs
Within which some such truth must lie
That can decipher empty cries
From empty bones
These fractured thoughts
From choices once an afterthought
And taut the purse-strings to enfold
A life still worthy of one's hold

To carry forth in hope for more
Than empty sky and barren shore
With chance again to be in grace
Fulfilled, with purpose, bold in place

And peace, and peace
Again, again
Be with me now
Eternal friend

And bind the wounds for forward step

Be with me, pray
Be with me yet

I

Though I falter
I give
Though I fragment
I reside
Though I fall
I find, and forget
I am

Though I fear
I stand
Though I fatigue
I resolve
Though I fade
I glow in the love
I am

Enough

When light's closed door
Awakes no more

When moonrise sets
To still, healed regrets

When down path's song
As light blends long

To dust, ground wakes
With air, time takes

To silence sound bestows
Goodness only knows

That round corner's bend
True intent treads and tends

To love, honour calls
Imbued in us all

As time will unfold
Journey's end told

And with, truth and love
We ascend, when enough

Departure

Opportunity beckons
I gravel out
Through lids, ivy coated
Struggling to lift their weight
Soaked, hacked, strained

I see myself dance
Through scenes, long forgotten
Rising from febrile fogs
Fatigued beyond compare
And yet I dance with
Soul unencumbered
Revisiting the mundane
Magnificent in waltzes and swirls
Choreographed to perfection
Somehow.

Ivy's gravity pulls
I hadn't prepared for this foliage
So steadily it replaces
While I move on, lightly
Knowing its greenery will be not
The final garden I'll grace

Dear One

In gladness
Fall heavy of lid
Pray peace
Succour the silence
Forever free, amongst clouds
Charging soul
With tidal strength

Give in
Pull out, long into the tow of great unknown

Going mercifully
In hand
With grace

All's Well

For every step to'
My limbs quake

In every joy felt
Old edges soften

In memories shared
My burden lightens

In tears shed
I am relief

With hope's smallest sign
My heart awakens

With fear's subtlest give
I can fly

In heart's yearned forgiveness
I am free

To sun's remembrance
I release

Open

Lighten
Wash away
Give to streams of time

Know thyself
As ripple, within
Diffusing to, and fro
Colour to tone
Unique, grown
Fulfilling,
Fulfilled

At the close, open
To beyond

Horizons

The end is nigh
I saw it written
In clouds, and lullabies

I myself am taken
Given over to chariots
Of sun
And moon
Too soon?
No
That'd be mistaken

Softly it sounds
Sweetly smoothing the way
A blend of night starry
And crisp autumnal display, daylight
Breaking
Across horizon's new
Supper sublime partaken

Grace, free,
To music's air and song
No, not forsaken,
But granted
Compassionately

Long, awaited,

Long

Antiphon

To leave you
Behind
Is pain
Beyond bearing

Call to me
And I will
Listen

And in that
Space
Between breath
And despair

Feel my
Answer
As love
And love
And love

Flow

Flow, flow over
Be not in wait
Flow!

Give, in currents
Full freedom, for purpose unknown

Abide, graciously
In balance, reserve
Yield as stem to squall
Fear befall
Torrents withstand
In solitude, quiet

Merging haem to water
Falling in pattern, unseen

Move, alight, guided
By cues, silent breaths
Leaning weights
To follow light and bend wing
In might bestowed
Higher through

Set

I feel the steady pull of fate
Casting my irons
Westbound
To set

Traversing
Field 'n' glen
Peak 'n' side
Sundering
Shadows to
Smoke to wind
To timings
Forgotten

This polka's
Persistent
Existence

Extraordinary
Plain
Moving to gain
My time
Come
To pass

Slip Switch

Step to past
Lines of time
Tracks blurred
In frames merged with thought, feeling
Unchanged,
Newly seen

Clicking tracks to expand one's nature
Extract one's purpose
And stand in sight
Intoned forward

Bridging tracks
Connecting streams
Known to body, place

Give, forgive
Release to rhythms
Onward

In light, enlightened
In love

Call

I hear
The rolling tide
Of distant shores

Beckoning

Harkening to my
Changing

Rolling nearer

To Dream

Through fields I glide
Suspended in tip's touch
Crowns in wheaten light
Golden breath
Drawn through dell's inhalation
To surge symphonic
Rise to rise
Breaching ridge
To tomorrow

In life's

Golden

End is

Always

Love

The author

Watkins is a Kiwi and works in general practice in Northland.

www.ingramcontent.com/pod-product-compliance
Lightning Source LLC
Chambersburg PA
CBHW051437290426
44109CB00016B/1595

9780473602772